WAKIN' UP WAGGIN'

The Tale Behind the Tail

WRITTEN BY ERIKA LEBLING   ILLUSTRATED BY JENNIFER KRENTZ

Timmy did not want to get out of bed.
He pulled up his covers and buried his head.
The day was sunshiney; birds sang *la dee doo*,
Still Timmy felt grumpy and groggy and blue.

"Out of bed, Sleepyhead," called his mom from downstairs,
But Timmy rolled over and played unawares.
Then came a sound that he couldn't ignore.
Something was thumping and bumping the floor.

He lifted his quilt just enough to peer out
And came nose to nose with a cold, dewy snout.
The snout was attached to a big, burley hound
Whose tail was the source of the curious sound.

"Oh, Max," Timmy said. "I don't mean to be rude,
But can't you be quiet? I'm in a bad mood."
Still Max kept on wagging with gusto and glee.
He'd woken up happy as happy can be.

Acknowledging nothing could stop Max's tail,
The young boy then asked, "Max, why must your tail flail?"
Max jumped on the bed, and he licked Timmy's face.
"I can't help it. My world is a wonderful place!

The first sight of my day is my very best friend.

I love hearing birds singing into the wind.

I never get cold with these thick, shaggy locks.

I'm fast like a cheetah

and strong like an ox."

This morning repeated each day after day—
Tim waking up grumpy; Max eager to play.

The days turned to months and then months multiplied,
And Timmy and Max both grew up side by side.

The boy and his pup, now a man and his dog,
Went out one fine day for a leisurely jog.
Max's body was tired, his muzzle was gray,
But the mutt wagged along, prompting Timmy to say,

"You're long in the tooth. You're no longer a kid.
Your eyes do not see me as well as they did.
You barely can hear. Your thick hair's falling out.
So I'm wondering *now* what you're wagging about."

Timmy knelt down, and then Max licked his face
And told him, "I *still* live in a wonderful place!
You're right that my sight's not as good as it was,
But I don't need my eyes to feel your belly rubs.

I do miss the sound of birds'
songs in my ears,
But their smell on the wind
lets me know that they're near.

Thin hair keeps me cool
when I nap in the shade.
I'm telling you, Timmy,
I've got this life made!"

Timmy considered all Max had described
And felt something shifting way deep down inside.
He'd learned from his friend in this one brief exchange
That gratitude brings about attitude change.

He understood now, that no matter what,
Each day would be good for this glass-half-full mutt.
Like a spark in the dark, an epiphany came:
If Max woke up wagging, could he do the same?

"Oh Max! Tim exclaimed. "I want to wag, too!
So starting today, I will follow your cue.
I'll live in the moment, give thanks as I should
For all that I have that makes my life good.

I'll sing with the birds and enjoy this fun ride,
And if a storm comes, I'll look on the bright side.
But wait, Max! I realized I'm missing one thing!
Unlike you, I don't have a tail I can swing!"

"I'm proud of you, Timmy, for making this choice.
You don't need a tail. You can wag with your voice!
With a clap of your hands, lean your head back and say:
By gosh! It is going to be a great day!"

From that moment on, through the good and the bad,
Tim woke up "wagging" with all that he had.
Some days it felt harder, and that was ok.
He'd just think of his dog, and ask, "What would Max say?"

He'd say,

"If you wake up feeling down and can't manage a grin,
Remember good feelings can come from within.
Take a deep breath, hold it in, then exhale.
Think of one tiny thing that tickles your tail.

Listen for birds singing *la dee dee do*.
Imagine they're singing that song just for you.
Before long, you'll feel even better than great
Because *happy* is something that you can create!

So take the lemons of life and make lemonade,
Go on adventures or nap in the shade,
Wag your tail lots, lick your friends in the face,
And *your* world will be the most wonderful place!"

And with Max's inspiring words in his head,
Tim would throw back his covers and spring out of bed.
He was Wakin' Up Waggin' and ready to play.
"By gosh!" he would howl. "It's going to be a great day!"

Epilogue

Today Timmy lives the most wonderful life!
He has two perfect kids and a pretty cool wife.
Their laughter and love fill their home to the brim,
And they all live by lessons that Max taught to Tim.

As for Max, the big mutt with the spirited tail,
After seventeen years, he packed up and set sail.
He now lives on the moon, all surrounded by stars,
So his family can see him wherever they are.

For Timmy and our two perfect kids, all of whom make my tail wag
-E.L.

I'd like to thank my wonderful niece for inviting me along on this fun ride.
-J.K.

A NOTE FROM THE AUTHOR

While this story is inspired by a very real friendship between a man and his dog, it is largely a work of fiction. For example, has Timmy ever been that grumpy? No, never! And when Timmy and Max talked to each other in real life, did they always do so in four-line rhyming stanzas? Probably not. Although, I wouldn't put it past them.

I'd also like to thank my talented aunt Jennifer Krentz for bringing Max back to life on these pages. I learned from her at an early age that life is always better with dogs, and that lesson has made all the difference.

Library of Congress Control Number: 2022920108
Hardcover: 979-8-9871821-0-9
Paperback: 979-8-9871821-1-6
Ebook: 979-8-9871821-2-3

Text copyright © Erika Lebling
Illustrations copyright © Jennifer Krentz
Book design by Derek Marantz Designs
www.DerekMarantz.com

Follow @erikaleblingwrites and @jenniferkrentzart for more stories and art.

WHAT TICKLES *YOUR* TAIL?

Gratitude List

_____

_____

_____

_____

_____

_____

_____

_____

Lightning Source UK Ltd.
Milton Keynes UK
UKHW051126071222
413453UK00003B/23